Homophobia

I0411960

The Ultimate Guide for How to Overcome Homophobic Thoughts Forever

within is the solitary and utter responsibility of the recipient reader. Under no circumstances will any legal responsibility or blame be held against the publisher for any reparation, damages, or monetary loss due to the information herein, either directly or indirectly.

The information herein is offered for informational purposes solely, and is universal as so. The presentation of the information is without contract or any type of guarantee assurance.

The trademarks that are used are without any consent, and the publication of the trademark is without permission or backing by the trademark owner. All trademarks and brands within this book are for clarifying purposes only and are the owned by the owners themselves, not affiliated with this document.

Table Of Contents

Introduction

The pages in this short, concise book were developed through years of experiences that I have gone through, as well as what has proven to work for the others that I have researched and talked to. I also want to congratulate you for taking the time to understand your own homophobia and how you can overcome it, not only for yourself but also for the people you are dealing with in everyday life.

After experiencing many different types of fears throughout my life and struggling to overcome them, I decided that I wanted to write a short, detailed book to help other people who are in a similar situation as I was. I also wanted to help people understand how homophobia forms and why people experience it, because there are people who may have relatives or friends that are homosexual and find themselves unable to relate. More importantly, it is important to understand the causes and solutions to homophobia not only for one to be able to relate to homosexual relatives and friends, but also to be able to understand them and accept them for who they are.

You will find this book useful if you make sure to implement what you learn in the following pages. The important thing is that you IMPLEMENT what you learn. Homophobia is not conquered overnight but the important thing to remember is that it is definitely possible for you to overcome it. The information in this book is aimed at helping you better understand your own mind and thought patterns.

Every person has had different experiences in their lives that work to develop their worldview. The unfortunate thing is that many people were raised to believe that homosexuals are bad people who make poor choices. Sometimes these people realize later on in their life that they carry some negative beliefs around with them still. As you go through these pages, you'll get a better understanding of what homophobia really is, where it comes from, and you will learn several ways that you, or others, can overcome it.

We will dive into what is going on in your brain, how your body reacts to your triggers, how your early childhood can influence the way you look at others, as well as what work is required of you to get past the roadblocks you have.

It is recommended that you take notes while you are reading this book. This will ensure that you get the most out of the information in here. The notes will help you to pinpoint exactly what you need to implement and by writing things down, you will be able to recall specifics and how to handle certain situations when they arise.

Lastly, remember that everything in this book has been compiled through research, my own experiences, as well as the experiences of others, so feel free to question what you have read in this book. It is encouraged that you do your own research on the topics you want to look deeper into. The more you understand about your own mind and society, the better off you'll be. To overcome a fear in your life, it will take some work on your part but you can do it! So remember to read with confidence and an open mind!

Chapter 1:

What Is Homophobia?

Generally speaking, homophobia is the fear or hatred for homosexuals. By homosexuals, we mean gay men and lesbians as the primary target of this condition. This fear most often leads to expressions of disgust, hostility, as well as some acts of violence.

Homophobia is something that can be found in people of any age, from all walks of life, and is not confined to one sector of the community. There are organized hate groups that exist today which aim at attacking, harassing, or bringing down the esteem of homosexuals through the use of violent language or through non-verbal actions such as insulting stares, or even through certain discriminatory policies that prevent homosexuals from enjoying the same kinds of services as the rest of the general population. These are usually done in attempts to intimidate or persecute them.

Many psychologists have analyzed homophobia. It has been referred to as an "irrational hatred or fear of homosexuality", normally directed at other people but can also be directed at one's self. This so-called target of homophobia – either at other people or towards oneself – can be better understood as the different types of homophobia are discussed in this chapter.

Types of Homophobia

Homophobia can be divided into four types. These four divisions are inter-related types of the same condition: personal homophobia, interpersonal homophobia, institutional homophobia and cultural homophobia. We will look at each of these subdivisions in the following pages and see how they affect homophobia as a whole.

It is important to remember that homophobia is often deep-rooted and by understanding these four types of homophobia, it will be easier for one to pinpoint his/her own beliefs and how they developed to become what they are.

Personal Homophobia

Personal homophobia can also be referred to as "Internalized Homophobia". This is a particular prejudice that is based on the belief that homosexuals in general are immoral, sinful, and inferior to heterosexuals. Some people even believe that homosexuality is a mental illness, and people who claim to be homosexual are suffering.

This can manifest itself in a person through feelings of dislike, discomfort, fear, disgust or hatred towards homosexuals. Regardless of sexual orientation or preference, anybody can go through personal homophobia to some extent.

The sources of personal homophobia are complex – it may either be caused by the personal environment that one lives in, such as one's immediate family and relatives, or it may also be brought about by the different groups of people that one socializes with, such as homophobic groups as well. This is why personal or internalized homophobia is a complicated matter and the means to overcome it usually requires at least knowing where the personal feelings of dislike are stemming from.

When people fear those who belong to the LGBT community, the term for the condition is internalized homophobia. Just like their heterosexual counterparts, many gays, bisexuals, and lesbians have also been taught in their childhood that homosexuals are inferior to heterosexuals. When this is taught at a very young age, it is often internalized to the point where it becomes hard for gays, lesbians, or bisexuals to accept their true sexuality.

Once homophobia has been internalized, it becomes difficult not only for heterosexuals who would always believe that they are superior, but it also increases the burden of LGBT people because it adds to their discomfort that they are unwanted. A common result of this is the desperate denial of some of the LGBT people, which leads to serious damage to their self-esteem, and could even lead to self-hatred or suicide.

In many instances, homophobic beliefs make people act in accordance to their prejudice regardless of if it is at work, clubs, in school, or any other place. In turn, these beliefs often lead homophobic people to believe that they are superior in all aspects of life. Research has proven that bias against homosexuals is much more accepted amongst Americans (not to single out the country, as many, many countries have the same reality) than bias against other minority groups.

As the human race has developed, it is part of many cultures to try and feel superior to others. We often find ourselves trying to find something that is unique to each one of us in order to gain confidence in ourselves. This is often the reason why people who tend to show hatred towards homosexuals even blame them for the problems caused in the society they share.

Sometimes, homophobic people blame homosexuals and their so-called inability to 'cure' their illness. It also happens that homophobic people push homosexuals to have themselves checked by a psychological expert in order to 'cure' their homosexuality. These acts just show that it is easier for them to blame another group who is different than them, than to accept that both groups could be part of the problem. Instead of owning up to one's mistakes and collectively moving forward to formulate a solution, personal homophobia leads to an endless blame game that does not lead to conflict resolution at all.

Interpersonal Homophobia

Interpersonal homophobia as a behavior can usually be associated with personal homophobia. Hatred for homosexuals is expressed through the use of name-calling, physical and verbal harassment, telling jokes that use homosexuality or LGBT people as topics, and other acts of discrimination. In its most extreme, this type of homophobia can result in the physical assaulting of LGBT people, simply because of fear and/or superiority complex.

In other cases, people with interpersonal homophobia act out their fear towards LGBT people in more commonplace and nonviolent methods such as shunning LGBT family members, becoming distant and cold towards co-workers and colleagues who are LGBT, and being uninterested in hearing or talking about the relationships of their LGBT friends.

This is more common and unfortunately, it is common for a homosexual to have at least 1 friend or family member become distant with them after they come out. The friend or family member often will not admit that they are separating themselves, however, it is usually shown when topics regarding personal life come up in conversation between them.

While interpersonal homophobia may be expressed in both verbal and non-verbal ways, each of these two methods are hurtful all the same. It makes no difference whether a homophobic person lets out insults to a friend or a relative who is a member of the LGBT community, or this person deliberately ignores or leaves the LGBT person out of a conversation. In these latter examples, it is quite unfair for the LGBT person because he or she is being shunned and is being robbed of the opportunity to make substantive contributions just because of his/her sexual orientation.

Institutional Homophobia

Institutional homophobia generally refers to the actions of institutions such as the government, churches, businesses, organizations, and others that discriminate against people on the basis of their sexual orientation. Another term for this kind of homophobia is heterosexism.

Effects of this type of fear are commonly reflected in religious institutions that have strictly implied rules and policies that act against gays, lesbians, bisexuals and trans-genders from leading/attending religious services. The type of institutional homophobia that exists among organized religious groups is one of the most difficult ones to overcome, both at the personal and at the institutional level.

At the personal level, it is difficult for a person who is an avid believer of a particular homophobic religion to go against this group's beliefs, out of fear of being excommunicated or judged by the people sharing the same religion.

At the institutional level, no matter how much the members of the religious group want to accept and accommodate homosexual people, there are certain difficulties along the way – such as traditions, norms, and the disapproval of the elders or those who occupy high positions within the group. Among these, it is most difficult to go against a particular religion's 'sacred teachings' just to accommodate homosexual people. Thus, members of the institution are left with no choice but to adopt and exercise the same kind of beliefs.

This institutional homophobia is also reflected in particular companies and agencies which deny allocating service resources to LGBT people, and in governments which fail to ensure the rights of all of its citizens, regardless of gender or sexual orientation. This type of homophobia is becoming much less common, as we have progressed as a society (for most of the world).

Many hundreds of years ago, homosexuals were stoned, beaten, and even killed by members of religious institutions because of their sexual orientation. These days, the same religious institutions are no longer committing these extreme hate crimes on homosexuals (at least in most parts of the world).

As compared to the institutional homophobia in religious groups or organizations, this type of homophobia that is perpetuated among the workplace is easier to overcome, since these discriminatory policies may be easily overturned and are not set in stone unlike religious teachings that have been passed on from generation to generation. These discriminatory policies may be overturned either through internal memorandums or in the case of government offices, through government pronouncements that will eventually provide equal access and opportunities to all.

As time has passed, some religions have even opened separate churches that are specifically for members who label themselves as gay, lesbian, bisexual, or trans-gender. These would not have even been talked about a couple hundred years ago and it shows that societies in our present day are becoming much more tolerant to these members, even if it might contradict the words in the holy book they believe in.

Aside from that, certain little but meaningful institutional changes such as common bathrooms for both male and female (so that gays and/or lesbians will no longer be discriminated for entering the "wrong" bathroom) as well as gender-neutral pronouns such as "Mx." instead of "Mr." and "Ms." are small steps towards overcoming institutional homophobia. It's important to remember that large societal and cultural changes are hard to notice in our day to day lives. But when we compare changes by the decade, we can surely notice progression in our current Western society.

Cultural Homophobia

Cultural homophobia refers to the norms and standards of a society, which dictate heterosexual dominance over being LGBT, often saying that being heterosexual is more moral or superior, and that everyone in the society should strive to be heterosexual because it is "better".

At one point, this was basically spelled out in almost all forms of media, from print advertisements to television shows. This involves only having heterosexual characters; erotic relationships being only between males and females, and every child that is described as "normal" will be presumed to be attracted to and will marry someone of the opposite sex. The causes and effects of cultural homophobia may be related to institutional homophobia – sometimes, a particular country's culture is affected by the majority religion being practiced in that country, thus influencing the way that its citizens look at LGBTs.

In the very few instances when LGBTs are featured, they are usually portrayed as people engaged in self-destructive behaviors, unhappy, or lesser in other ways. A common example of cultural homophobia portrayed through the media would be homosexual men characterized as being feminine and/or dressing in very colorful clothing all the time.

Another common example of LGBT portrayal in television shows or movies would be LGBT people being portrayed as a third-party hindrance to a heterosexual couple's relationship. In countries wherein religion is a huge influencer to culture, television shows featuring legal homosexual relationships are often censored. This is a clear manifestation of cultural homophobia. Moreover, intimate scenes between people of the same sex are often edited out or not included at all in these types of television shows.

Many homosexuals become angry at this type of characterization because it may only represent a small percentage of the gay community, and in fact, most heterosexual men dress in the same type of outfit that a heterosexual man would dress in. This kind of characterization does not only happen to gay men, but also to lesbians. Some television shows like to portray lesbians as women trying to dress up in traditionally male attire and putting up a macho act, when in fact, not all lesbians act that way. Some, if not most, lesbians dress up the same way as straight women. The only way you would know that these men or women are homosexuals is if they were to tell you their sexual orientation.

The reason many homosexuals may become angry at such examples portrayed in the media is because it often is shown as the butt of jokes. Maybe by showing a gay male as very weak compared to a straight male or a female who claims to be lesbian as being confused and in denial, or looking for attention. Again, some of these examples could be true, but it doesn't represent the overwhelming majority of the homosexual population.

Moreover, having these types of characterizations shown in mainstream media – particularly in popular and primetime television shows – just further deepens the discrimination against homosexuals. These types of characterizations do not help in educating the people about homosexuals not being evil people, but they further perpetuate the hateful treatment towards LGBTs.

It should be noted however, that cultural homophobia seems to be disappearing rapidly in the mainstream media. Shows like Glee and Modern Family are some of the most popular shows on television and openly gay characters play an integral role in them.

This phenomenon of openly gay character roles in movies and television shows are becoming fairly common and seem to be accepted by the general public, based on the ratings being garnered. These factors, combined with it becoming "politically incorrect" to portray homosexuals in the media in a negative light, figures to drastically reduce cultural homophobia even further in the next few decades.

But then again, having gay people portrayed correctly without being discriminated in these television shows is just one step towards reducing cultural homophobia. One must look at the more complex picture of cultural homophobia in a particular country, especially if these beliefs stem from long-time traditions or religious   norms.

Chapter 2:

Causes of Homophobia

The reasons why people can become homophobic vary depending on which type, or types, of homophobia they have. Now that we understand the four inter-related subdivisions of homophobia, we will now go into the causes for each and how they affect each other.

Personal Homophobia

Unfortunately, the majority of the time, personal homophobia is caused by misinformation. Just like in the cases of sexism and racism, people can be taught to become homophobic. Myths concerning the LGBT community are perpetuated in society even with the apparent lack of credible and accurate information about them.

Many children are also given biased information about the LGBT community and aren't able to develop their own opinions until they already have a firm mindset of how to view homosexuals. This phenomenon can also be referred to as "confirmation bias", where instead of judging situations/people with an open mind, we see what we choose to see based on conclusions that we have already developed (or have been developed by our elders and instilled in us).

As you might have guessed by now, misinformation about homosexuality and the stereotypes learned from childhood are carried on into adulthood. This may be greatly affected by the kind of surroundings that a child grows up in. If he/she is raised in an open-minded family, then there are more chances that the child would be more open and tolerating to homosexuals.

On the other hand, if the child grew up in an environment wherein people are strictly homophobic, the chance that this way of thinking will be carried on into adulthood is that much greater. Moreover, the child will have a difficult time trying to separate his/her own beliefs from the beliefs of the people in the environment. Much more than that, the child may have a hard time expressing his/her dissenting views, especially if he/she supports homosexuals.

Promotion of lies about homosexuality by religious institutions also contribute to the development of personal homophobia. This was already discussed in the previous chapter – and it was also said earlier that homophobia perpetuated by religion is difficult to overcome because of the layers of traditions that one has to go against if ever he/she chooses to believe otherwise.

Often times, you will notice that someone who is very homophobic has never tried to befriend a homosexual at any time during their life. They may have learned at a young age to look down upon homosexuals, but because they never tried to befriend or understand a homosexual, they were never able to overcome this communication block. As you can see, it becomes a cycle that perpetuates itself.

It may also be the case when homophobic people establish acquaintances or friendships with homosexuals, but would easily turn their back on them once things get rough. Examples of these kinds of people are those who assert that they have homosexual friends but refuse to defend them in fighting for their rights.

Likewise, many people who were exposed to the LGBT community in their early childhood, teenage years, or early twenties can become very understanding of gay rights and sometimes become some of the biggest supporters of the movement. These are the types of people who are often construed to be members of the LGBT community as well because of their supportive stance, but what others fail to understand is that one does not necessarily have to be a member of the LGBT community in order to join them in their struggles.

Aside from exposure to the LGBT community, the support coming from these people often stems from deeper and more personal matters – it might be experiences with family members having trouble coming out as gay, or it might be due to having friends who are LGBTs that have suffered from hate crimes and the like.

When it comes to the cause of personal homophobia, it is important to remember that there is usually a strong correlation between exposure to homosexuality and homophobia. In essence, the more a person is exposed to personal contact with homosexuals, the more understanding they become towards them. Though obviously not always the case, this rings true the vast majority of the time.

It can often be noticed that those who have family members – especially immediate family members like brothers or sisters – who are LGBTs are more sensitive to their needs and are more willing to fight for their rights. In this case, it is difficult to overcome personal homophobia since deep personal experiences are also required in order to open one's mind to their struggles.

Interpersonal Homophobia

Along with prejudice, the cause of this particular type of homophobia can be explained by linking other psychological factors. People with interpersonal homophobia, who oftentimes are not comfortable with their own sexuality, try to force a "correct" sexual mindset onto members of the LGBT community. By forcing this heterosexual mindset, they are able to feel better about their own confusion and it gives them a strong sense of character because they feel as if they have helped cure the "wrong" in the world.

The causes of interpersonal homophobia can usually be traced back to a strong feeling of personal homophobia. When a person has developed very deep negative emotional anchors to homosexuality, that person is much more likely to commit acts of interpersonal homophobia. Most people who are personally homophobic will not commit acts of interpersonal homophobia unless they have a strong hatred towards homosexuals or if they are in a group of like-minded individuals. This kind of strong hatred against homosexuals is often irrational and its cause cannot be easily traced.

Unfortunately, this can be seen when heterosexuals try to use odd reasons to interact with homosexuals. There are countless occurrences when a straight person (almost always men in recorded instances) will open a "gay conversion therapy" or try to "fix" homosexuals. It appears that in the vast majority of these situations, the person behind the idea seems to be someone who has repressed his homosexual feelings.

It can be the case wherein the homophobic person is attempting to "fix" homosexuals to "test" if the method will work, especially if he/she is trying to repress his/her own homosexuality. This strong denial and lack of acceptance of one's true identity might lead a person to explore different ways to redirect his homosexual feelings and convince himself/herself that he/she is straight and that homosexuality is a matter of the mind.

Needless to say, sometimes the attempts to "fix" homosexuality may go too far. There was even an infamous case of an Iowa pastor who was found guilty of sexually harassing many young boys. He claimed that he was "raping the gay away" and that by partaking in those actions, he was trying to "remove their homosexual urges from them". Though this is an extreme case, these types of odd claims are usually the result of questionable homosexual men trying to privately "cure" others.

Again, this does not only apply to homosexual men. Some homosexual females can also be victims of this so-called "curing", wherein lesbians are forced upon either by their relatives or friends to act more "feminine". Sometimes, homosexual women actually force themselves into relationships with straight men in the hopes of having their feelings for fellow women be replaced by feelings for straight men, thus removing their homosexuality and reverting them back to straight women.

Institutional Homophobia

Institutional homophobia is, in part, caused by a competition for power between large institutions. Societies, like the one we live in now, create things such as scapegoats, which act to maintain the positions of those in power as well as the status quo. In this century alone, different groups such as African Americans, Jews, Muslims, Christians, Latin Americans, American Indians and LGBT people have been blamed for many problems, both economically and socially.

The institutional homophobia is propagated by different institutions, depending on the location in the world. For example, if you were to live in the Middle East, the institutions that are in power in those countries could influence you. This may promote an Islamic superiority and institutions that oppose it may be looked down upon as "wrong". Likewise, if you lived in the

United States, you could be influenced more by Christian values and view institutions that oppose these values as "wrong".

Not all members of institutions like Christianity or Islam view other institutions' ideals as inferior, but as mentioned in Chapter 1, we tend to want the culture we identify with to be better, or "more correct" than the others. This can be seen even in sports, businesses, or college rivalries. Wanting to be better than others is a core part of our mental development as a species and, in turn, our culture.

It is important to remember that institutional homophobia is largely dependent on what part of the world you live in, what institutions you choose to be a part of, as well as how those institutions view homophobia. This is not meant to bash religion or promote a secular point of view, but rather to help people who grew up religious, to understand where they may have developed their belief systems from and whether they consciously chose to be a part of those belief systems or if they were just a product of the environment they happened to be born into.

Cultural Homophobia

Cultural homophobia is largely caused by social norms that teach which sexuality is "correct". In a lot of cultures, sexual contact between people of the same sex has been widely accepted and practiced. This can often be seen in tribal cultures and also in ancient cultures. However, in the Western civilization, this type of sexual contact and homosexuality in general in repressed, except for the types needed for procreation. Same-sex sexuality therefore is damned and feared by many. Match this fear of same-sex sexuality with Western religious norms and you will have a society that is naturally homophobic.

An example of this would be that it is oftentimes looked down upon for a gay or lesbian couple to hold hands in public, whereas if a heterosexual couple were to do the same, it may not questioned. And then again, the same thing happens in scenes in television shows. Intimate scenes between homosexual couples, or sometimes even mere admission that a homosexual relationship exists, are often regarded as taboo while abusive, erotic, or other intimate scenes between heterosexual couples are allowed. As with many other aspects of life, these norms vary depending on where one lives - from the socially liberal to the socially conservative.

Misinformation

After enumerating the different types of homophobia and their possible causes, these causes might boil down to one thing: misinformation. First, homophobia is spread because of misconceptions about homosexuals and homosexuality. A common misconception is that homosexuality is an illness and can therefore be cured. It is not. Homosexuals are not "ill", they are as normal as straight people. Moreover, homosexuals are not inherently different from straight people – except for their preference of romantic partners.

Another common misconception against homosexuals is that they are all carriers of sexually-transmitted diseases (STDs). This strong accusation breeds disbelief and even disgust among homophobes, and it is wrong to think as such. Through simple research, it can be found out that STDs and other deadly diseases are not caused by one's sexual orientation. Moreover, these diseases can be transmitted from person to person and can infect people regardless of their gender orientation. Being homosexual has nothing to do with the spread of diseases, therefore there is the need to correct this kind of thinking.

Second, misinformation occurs when people spread false images of homosexual people. Some of the examples already mentioned are the ways that they are portrayed in mainstream media – gay men trying hard to be feminine, lesbian women trying hard to be macho. These stereotypes are not helpful at all, and the way to correct them is to make homophobic people realize – again and again – that one's sexual orientation does not automatically require a change in behavior.

A gay man may portray himself just like a straight man and there is no problem with that. With this kind of misinformation, not only must we correct personal misconceptions but there must also be steps to correct institutional misconceptions especially in workplaces or in communities.

Third, there is a stark spread of misinformation regarding the ability of heterosexuals to accept homosexuals. Some people believe that by accommodating homosexuals, one becomes homosexual as well. This is not true. Spreading this kind of information just deepens the hate against LGBTs and further distances people from understanding LGBT people and their struggles.

A heterosexual trying to overcome his/her homophobia by understanding the plight of LGBT people is not an automatic gateway to one's conversion to homosexuality. This is an incorrect and an illogical connection that people need to stop perpetuating. It is much more present in men, in which macho individuals do not want to give off the perception that they could be gay, thereby being proactive in letting others know they are not gay and attempt to limit interactions with gay men in their day to day life.

All in all, the spread of misinformation regarding homosexuals and homosexuality is outright dangerous as it may affect either personal, institutional, or cultural homophobia. This is why a constant and recurring theme in this book is the idea and importance of open-mindedness. With an open mind, one can debunk these wrong ideas and also make the necessary steps towards genuinely overcoming, not only personal homophobia, but others' as well.

Chapter 3:

Is There a Cure for Homophobia?

In some societies, homophobia is a pervasive condition. Since everyone is a product of society to some degree, many people living today can be considered as homophobic to some degree, regardless of beliefs or sexual orientation. You may assume that you are homophobic. The acknowledgement of homophobia's pervasive existence is the first requirement in constructively dealing with homophobia.

It is not an easy task to completely eradicate homophobic feelings, but if you are willing to acknowledge that you are homophobic, only then can you begin to take responsibility of your behavioral changes and choices in life. You can do the following:

Understanding Oppression

Reflect on the differences and similarities of homophobia and other types of oppression. Use the things that you know about sexism, racism, classism, and other types of elitist/discriminatory behavior that can be associated with oppression for you to better understand homophobia. It is important to understand that hundreds of years ago, slavery and sexism was considered "normal" to a large portion of the population.

Now, it is overwhelmingly agreed upon that slavery and sexism are immoral in many ways. Likewise, think about whether homophobia is the correct mindset to have if you were to live right now, hundreds of years ago, or two hundred years into the future. This will help to give you perspective and to stay out of all the cultural influences going on around you.

Moreover, try to put yourself in the shoes of a homosexual person and begin to imagine how you would feel if the same oppressive and discriminatory policies were directed towards you.

Homophobic women must understand that women did not have the same rights as men before. Women had to fight for the civil liberties and rights that they have at present, and thus, by being homophobic, they may try imagining themselves to be in the same oppressed condition as homosexuals. Before, women were regarded as the inferior gender, much the same as how society is treating homosexuals now. Having this kind of deep understanding about oppression, how it is perpetuated, and its lingering effects will enable a person to effectively let go of his/her homophobic stances.

Promotion

Aside from understanding how oppression looks and feels, it is also important to understand that homophobia is the problem and not homosexuality. Do not treat homosexuality as a sin because homosexuals have no say with what they're feeling. They are not ill, and most importantly, who in their right mind would choose to become homosexual if they knew all along that there would be many people discriminating against them? Rather, their sexuality is a given and not a disease, it is something that they did not choose but are willing to accept and fight for.

When talking to colleagues or friends, speak out regarding homophobia, if the topic comes up. For a lot of people, the only time that they talk about things concerning LGBT is when they are the subject of "jokes" or insults, or in private. Promoting acceptance for homosexuals can also be done by making homophobic people understand oppression as well, and also by making them understand that homosexual people have feelings too.

Promotion is also important in another way, because when you verbally say that a thing is correct, your mind is more likely to hold on to that as truth. This is why affirmations are so powerful in the self-development world. The more you talk about the problems regarding homophobia out loud and in public, the quicker you will be able to overcome it. Not only is promotion helpful for overcoming one's own homophobic beliefs, but it is also helpful to the many homophobic others who are misinformed about homosexuals.

Research

Research further on the experiences of people belonging to the LGBT community. Whether you are trying to overcome homophobia in order to better understand a family member or even if you don't know any homosexual people at all, it is important for you to become educated on how members of the LGBT community view certain topics.

By educating yourself on topics concerning the gay and lesbian community, you will be able to relate to the emotions behind the causes and it will give you a perspective that you did not previously have. Aside from that, researching on these kinds of topics will not only expand your understanding, but it will also expand your empathy. Again, this is especially for homophobic women who have also felt repressed or discriminated because of their sexual status.

Further efforts can be done by also encouraging yourself to support efforts for anti-discrimination, and also anti-homophobic violence and prejudice rallies and campaigns. In joining these efforts, one must maintain an open and determined mind. In itself, the battle against one's own homophobia is already hard to overcome, and it would require more effort to do so on a greater scale.

With that said, it is also important to listen to and read opposing viewpoints as well. Find some viewpoints from people that are homophobic and try to understand why they believe what they do. Put yourself in their shoes and try to feel the emotion and (possible) hatred that they feel. By doing this without judging them, you will find that you are able to relate to all sides better.

Moreover, by listening to both sides, you can formulate better responses to homophobic people's complaints, particularly because you know where they are coming from. However, you must be careful because attempting to make a person disregard his homophobic beliefs is a grueling task. It requires a lot of patience and may also pose risks to friendships and relationships.

Personal Experience

The most effective and quickest way to overcome homophobia is to try and befriend a person who is homosexual. By becoming friends with a person who is homosexual, you can get first-hand answers and observations that you will otherwise never have.

This is especially important if you were raised in an environment that frowned upon befriending someone who is LGBT. By learning about their experiences, not only can you disprove your previous discriminatory beliefs against the LGBT, but you can spread true information about homosexuality that may hopefully correct other people's mindsets.

Also, by being able to see that a person who has a different sexual orientation than you is just a normal person, you will better understand the gay and lesbian community as a whole. Moreover, by looking at homosexuals as normal people, you will understand that they are – in fact – just like you. The only difference between you and them is based on the sexual identity of the person that they have chosen to love and be attracted to. Aside from that, you are all the same and therefore there is nothing to discriminate or feel superior about.

Likewise, you could take a trip to the poorest country in the world and spend time in a village. In this experience, you might develop some compassion towards those who are less fortunate. Use this same principle when spending time with a homosexual. See if your experiences with them match up to what you were taught. Could you be friends with them based on their character? How are they different than you, other than what they do in their private life? Ask yourself, and them, these questions so that you can bridge the gap.

Change of Mindset

Combine the different strategies enumerated above – understanding oppression, promotion, research, and personal experience – all of these contribute to one very important way to overcome homophobia: changing one's mindset. Try to assess where your homophobic thoughts are coming from – are you repressing your own homosexual tendencies? Is your family homophobic? Is it from the environment that you live in? Is it because of your religion? Is it because of the culture perpetuated in society? Look at these various potential sources of homophobia, for they will greatly help in your attempt to change your mindset.

Changing your mindset towards homosexuals and homosexuality in general is not easy. At first, it might feel forced, that you are just trying to accept homosexuals but you still have inner reservations. This is a part of the process of opening your mind. But once you take that necessary step towards trying to understand homosexuals, you will realize that you have already unconsciously destroyed the walls that you have held up against them.

A change of mindset – that is, not looking at homosexuals as dirty or with disbelief – is beneficial not only for your own wellbeing, particularly your peace of mind and the stability of your relationships with other people, but it is helpful also to the people around you. Other people will only listen to their closest friends and/or relatives – and if they see that someone like you has opened their mind to the reality of homosexuality, then it is possible that you will also change other people's mindsets along the way.

Chapter 4:

Getting Rid of Homophobic Thoughts

Homophobic thoughts are set in the minds of a lot of people as they reach adulthood. One way to fight homophobic thoughts is by outgrowing them as if they are traumatic memories from childhood. Before you manage to get rid of something from inside of your system, you must first gain an understanding of what it is that you actually fear. Here are some simple steps that you can follow:

Origins

Find out where it began. Take a look back at your history and try to figure out what led to you having homophobic thoughts in the first place. Have there been people in your life that have been extremely homophobic? Have you encountered people who spoke negatively about LGBT people? They may either have consciously or unconsciously influenced you in some way. Try asking yourself why these people acted the way they did, as well as the reasons why you have accepted these beliefs to be true.

Sometimes, the origins of your homophobic thoughts may be within yourself. Aside from looking at your history and assessing your environment as to whether they have cultivated such thoughts, you may also try asking yourself if you have repressed homosexual feelings. Sometimes, the most homophobic people are those who deny that they are also homosexual.

Out of the fear of being judged or being "caught" as gay, these kinds of people put up a homophobic image so that no one would think that they are also the same as the people they purportedly hate.

It is not wrong to search for the origins of such thoughts. This exercise is not for you to locate the target of blame, but rather it is to locate the proper starting point towards eliminating homophobic thoughts within yourself.

Be Open-Minded

In order for you to understand homosexuality, the first thing you need to do is to allow your mind to see different paradigms. This does not necessarily mean that you should immerse yourself in homosexual activities or communities. Simply researching about the LGBT community can be a good start.

You can utilize materials such as the internet in order to find out how homosexuals act and behave in particular situations. The fear you feel towards them will slowly die down once you gain an understanding of how they live and what personalities they have.

Opening one's mind is not something that is usually done successfully at first attempt. It takes a lot of hard work, personal dedication, and emotional determination. Certain hindrances to being open-minded include the fear of being judged due to opinions and beliefs that go against the norm. Out of the fear of being ridiculed, there are times when one consciously and deliberately closes one's mind to the thought of accommodating homosexuals and settles at being homophobic instead.

One of the silliest reasons people give for not wanting to understand homosexuals is that they will become interested in partaking in homosexual acts by associating with them. This is almost comical because some of the people who are most comfortable in their sexuality are friends with homosexuals and are completely heterosexual.

Moreover, partaking in homosexual acts is not an automatic derivative of understanding and being supportive of the LGBT community. If one does such acts, then it is a personal choice and not a direct result of being open-minded about homosexuals. One must be careful about placing such kind of blame, because these acts are entirely voluntary and are not automatically attached to one's beliefs. Accepting homosexuals for who they are and being straight are two separate things – these two conditions can exist individually.

Communication

Talk to a person who is not homophobic. Often times, homophobic individuals have no idea how they should act when they are around homosexuals. Even when they are being insensitive or utmost discriminatory, homophobes would still think that they are only doing the "right thing" and that homosexuals deserve that kind of treatment because they are inferior and are not "normal".

Only someone who has no fear towards gays, lesbians or bisexuals can give you the knowledge of properly dealing with LGBT people. You may choose to talk to not only these kinds of people, but also to those who personally have homosexual friends and/or relatives. This latter characterization of people can definitely provide an accurate and non-biased account of how homosexuals behave, and you will realize that they are just like you. Moreover, these kinds of people can give you effective advice on how to deal, not only with your own homophobia, but also with other homophobic people.

So if you happen to have friends who have an open mind when it comes to the topic of sexual orientation, you can ask them about their views. Do not be afraid to ask questions, especially if getting the answers to these questions is the key towards your personal acceptance of homosexuals. Let these people tell you how they befriend and interact with homosexuals.

This can be invaluable, as they are actually a personal friend of yours who you already trust. Moreover, talking to someone you know personally whose experience you can definitely tag as credible has a different effect than merely reading strangers' viewpoints on the internet. Having a personal confidante on these kinds of thoughts is vital in overcoming homophobia.

Stop Negativity

Slowly separate yourself from negative homophobic acts and thoughts. Now that you are trying to stop being homophobic, you should also learn to stop making negative jokes and comments that are directed towards homosexuals, or any other minority, for that matter. It only reinforces the homophobic thoughts and will inhibit your mental development regarding acceptance. Do not tolerate, nor participate, when someone else starts these destructive conversations.

Learn to be more sensitive, especially when you are around LGBT friends and/or family members. When you hear people making fun of LGBTs, have the guts to correct them, but don't be too confrontational when going about it. If you cannot do so in public, you can always approach them in private. Although you may find this hard to do at first, you will slowly improve over time. And if you continuously do so, other people will soon realize that they must not make fun of homosexuals and homosexuality when you are around.

I want to point out that this does not mean you should become a person with no sense of humor who can't tease anyone in good nature. The key is that if you are going to poke fun at people, do it in a playful and non-hateful way. You know what your intentions are.

Having other people make fun of you behind your back is unpleasant, and if you keep this thought in mind, then you will have a more sensitive standpoint when it comes to LGBT remarks.

This chapter provided tips on how to overcome homophobia – and although the list may not be exhaustive, the tips listed here are necessary and are good starting points. Of course, the biggest tip is to be true to yourself. Without having pure intentions of overcoming homophobia, these tips will not work. Moreover, as you try your best to understand homosexuality better, you will realize that different people have different ways of overcoming homophobia. It may be a long and grueling task, but you will get there.

Envision the Greater Picture

Trying to get rid of homophobic thoughts and eventually overcoming homophobia as a whole is not a simple task – it is a lifelong change. Once you have successfully overcome your homophobic thoughts, almost everything will change: your personal disposition, the way you treat homosexuals, the way you interact with them, your personal beliefs on marginalized and oppressed groups in society, your personal sense of empathy and sensitivity, and basically how you will mingle with other people from that point forward.

This is why it is important – in everything that you do in this quest – that you envision the greater picture. This is in line with eliminating negative thoughts. Always ask yourself: what greater good will it bring if I stop being intolerant of homosexuals? How much better would my life and relationships be if I get rid of homophobic thoughts? What would my good deed mean to those suffering from discrimination and repression just because of their sexual orientation? If I were in their shoes, how would I feel about having the continuous struggle of trying to prove myself worthy of people's trust?

Ask yourself these questions and you will develop a greater sense of purpose with what you are doing. Remember that you are overcoming homophobia not only for yourself and not only to correct your mistakes, but also for the sake of the LGBT community. For them, the acceptance of one person means a lot and makes a lot of difference, because they are in that state wherein they have to struggle for their rights every single day and that they have to continuously convince people that they are worth accepting in society.

The acceptance of one person is precious in itself, how much more is the acceptance of society? Change must begin within the self first, and then once you have successfully done so, you may proceed towards introducing the same kind of change to your community and then to the greater society.

Chapter 5:

Physiology and Focus

Before we manage to get rid of homophobia, we must first understand how fear is created. Whatever you feel right now is the result of two intertwined factors: physiology and focus.

Physiology is defined as the way a person uses his/her body in all aspects. This includes the way you breathe, your posture, and even things like how active you have been, or whether you have been eating a lot of high-sugar foods, or vegetables.

Focus refers to the way you are using your mind. This includes your beliefs, what thoughts are running through your head, the way you describe yourself, and the language you are using when you are thinking.

Every single feeling that you experience in your day is the result of an exact or precise strategy made up of numerous combined elements of physiology and focus that you are using at that instance. The good news about this is that you have the power to change these strategies whenever you wish and in whatever form.

An example of this is depression (not clinical depression); although this is considered by many to be a big mystery, the condition can only be experienced when the patient follows an exact strategy for depression. When we compare the body language and thoughts of an emotionally healthy person to a depressed one, we would notice that depressed people often have their shoulders forward, head down, breathe in a shallow manner and constantly think about what's wrong with their life. They point their focus more on searching for evidence to support their feelings of negativity towards life, as well as asking themselves questions which produce answers that only add up to the main problem.

The key lies in the questions that you normally ask yourself. These include asking what would happen if not everything goes as planned, and the mind will generate possible answers, which will only make you feel worse. Asking how you will make something awesome or how others will benefit when you overcome an obstacle will change the way you feel. When you change your focus and physiology, the feeling also changes. It is virtually impossible for someone to be depressed, yet hold their head up high, breathe deeply, and feel grateful at the exact same moment.

You can apply these same principles to your homophobia and implement them each and every day. Focus on how we are all the same as people. We all suffer from our own personal demons and no matter what someone shows on the outside, they are never completely happy. Also, remember that you have the power to benefit each person you come into contact with, so focus on spreading a message of equality and freedom for everyone and before you know it, you will have changed your physiology.

Chapter 6:

Keep Homophobic Thoughts Out of Your Mind through Anchoring

DISCLAIMER:

The technique in this chapter is a bonus and it is not a necessity to overcome your homophobia, however, it has been proven to work to overcome bad habits and negative emotions.

Jumping around, singing the songs you love or running consistently will definitely shift your mood to a more positive tone, but you will need a strategy that is more discreet in order for you to deal with your homophobic thoughts when there are other people around. The answer to this is a technique called "Anchoring". This is a simple, yet effective, technique which aims at tapping in the automatic system of neurology dealing with linking experiences to feelings. You might not know this, but you have already experienced anchoring many times in your life.

The process works like this: when a unique event occurs in your life which brings you to an extremely emotional state, regardless of if it is good or bad, your nervous system makes a link between the two. For example, when you first fell in love, there might have been a song playing on the radio.

When that song played repeatedly during that time, you were brought to an almost euphoric state of being in love; and now, whenever that song plays again, you are brought back to that particular moment in time and the euphoric love comes rushing back to you. Or, it could also be experienced when you walk into a building and it brings you back to the feeling of going back to school, especially if the building you are entering bares any resemblance, such as the smell of the floor polish or the color of the stone façade.

In both of these cases, the same thing happens: your mind makes an anchor, or link, between a strong feeling (being back at school or feeling of love) and a very unique stimulus (a particular song or the floor polish smell).

The way for you to use the anchoring method in removing homophobic thoughts is to deliberately make a link between some sort of unique stimulus, something that you have control over and you can initiate whenever you wish, and a strong kind of confident and calm feeling that you want to have instead of homophobic thoughts. Then, the magical part comes next: whenever you think about homosexuality, you simply apply the stimulus and your mind will link them together, creating a new map for the emotions belonging to homosexuality.

This means that your mind will literally make new neural pathways, which connect the positive emotions to replace the old ones. The aim in doing this is to join together groups of extremely powerful and positive emotions that you can bring up whenever you need them, or in whatever time you wish. This means that if you are ever facing a situation where you would normally respond negatively, you can simply fire your mind anchor and your brain will recode the event with positive feelings, so it becomes a positive experience for you to handle.

Here is how to do it:

Think of a very positive state or emotion that you want to use as your anchor. Remember that whatever you choose needs to be a very positive emotion, something that can be regarded as good by everyone and not just you. You can choose strong, powerful, centered, calm, relaxed, or love as the feelings you wish to have.

Pick a specific body part where you will attach your anchor. Anchoring basically works by connecting powerful emotions to a very specific and unique stimulus. This means that your stimulus needs to be something that you can easily do, but not something that can happen in your everyday life. This can either be squeezing your non-writing hand into a very tight fist. This is unique because it is something that you do not do often, yet it is very easy to do even when you are around people.

You can do one of these three things:

Remember a time in your life when you felt that strong emotion. Imagine yourself floating back to that particular moment in time, explore that memory, and let yourself get immersed in the very sense of it, reminiscing in the sights, scents, smells, and taste that you experienced in that particular moment. Breathe these feelings to every part of your body and engage in the process again and again until the intensity of the feelings increase.

Create a state of mind dedicated to your chosen emotion. Increase its effect by thinking of situations and allow all the positive energy you feel to flow throughout your body.

Anchor your emotions in the moments of your life when you felt particularly happy or joyful. Moments when you were laughing, loving, running, and other related things can be used for this.

As your emotions reach their very peak, press on your anchor about five to ten times – simply make sure that your chosen stimulus is unique enough, yet easy to replicate. When your feelings reach their very strongest, apply your anchor five to ten times. This part is when you create your links to the nervous system between the feeling and the stimulus.

Let your emotions return back to normal. Do this again a few more times. Make sure to repeat the whole process in order for the anchor's power to become stronger. The more emotions you put in, the stronger the stimulus becomes.

Using your physiology and focus, you are creating these emotions every day. In order for you to change what you feel, you need to change the way you think and how you consciously use your   body.

Conclusion

I worked hard on creating the best guide for "overcoming homophobia" that I could. After finally overcoming my roadblocks, I wanted to give back to others. These are all the strategies and information that has worked for me, as well as others that I have talked to and researched.

If you stay consistent they will work for you as well. I am hopeful that this book was able to instill the idea that one must not only think about himself or herself, but most especially, one must think about the people being the target of hate (i.e. homosexual people) and the ones whose minds you can still change (i.e. other homophobic individuals). Be optimistic about your current situation and make small progress each day!

If you've learned anything from this book, share it with others. Thank you and good luck in your own journey!